SELF-CARE CATS

A coloring book about

self-love

Copyright © 2020 Soulpress

Concept by Jamie Flynn Ruben. No part of this book may be reproduced or used in any manner without written permission of the copyright owner except for the use of quotations in a book review.

Some pens and markers stain through paper.
To avoid bleed-through problems and frustration,
please place a sheet of paper underneath the
page you are currently coloring.

IT'S ME TIME!

Grab your colouring pencils, and let the fun begin because you're about to discover the wonderful world of self-care and self-discovery! Leading by example, your new furry cat friends will encourage you to slow down, relax, and show yourself some unconditional love. Light a candle, put your favourite song on, take a hot bubble bath, and get a good night's sleep. It's time to put yourself first and find joy in your day-to-day life. They say it's the little things that matter, right?

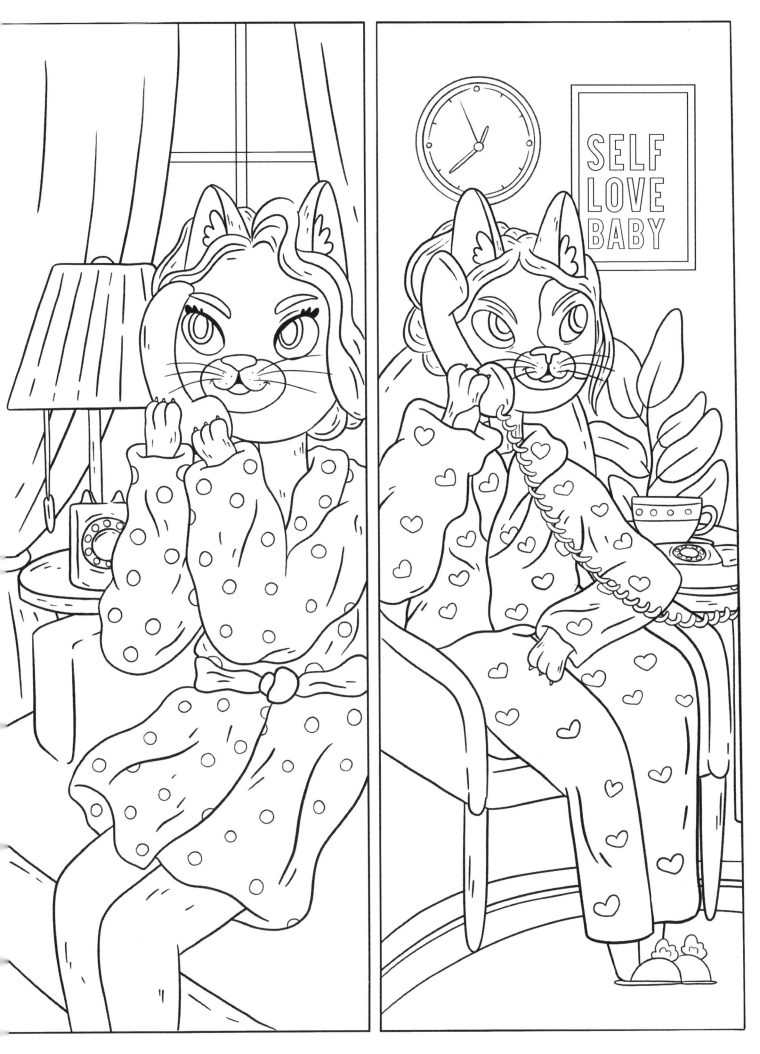

SELF-CARE IS...
Enjoying a nourishing breakfast

SELF-CARE IS...
Buying yourself something nice

SELF-CARE IS...
Getting a good night's sleep

Made in the USA
Las Vegas, NV
22 April 2022